TRAIN YOUR BRAIN LOGIC PUZZLES

Sharpen your logical reasoning skills and have fun with these engaging deduction puzzles.

Great for anyone who loves a good mental challenge!

Perfect for fans of brain teasers, creative thinking, and critical thinking games, each puzzle encourages you to make connections, analyze clues, and think flexibly.

Ideal for classrooms (a great fast finisher activity!), therapy sessions, or independent enrichment, these puzzles support executive function, reasoning, and problem-solving skills.

Puzzles created by three Speech Language Pathologists who specialize in Cognitive Rehabilitation Therapy. Look for the answer key at the end of the book.

Created by:

April Crystal MS, CCC/SLP

Emily Harrison MS, CCC/SLP

Michelle Huish MS, CCC/SLP

Helpful Hints for Completing Logic Puzzles

1. **Use all information:**
   All items and facts listed in the clues will be used somewhere in the puzzle.

2. **Identify pairs:**
   Look for items or facts that need to stay together.

3. **Use the graph:**
   Check the clues and the graph to see where items or facts can fit in the puzzle.

4. **Start easy:**
   Fill in the given items and facts first.

5. **Take breaks:**
   If you feel stuck, step away and come back with fresh eyes and a rested brain.

6. **Read aloud:**
   Sometimes hearing the clues helps you process the details.

7. **Mark used clues:**
   Cross off what you've already solved so you know what's done and what still needs your attention.

8. **Underline/highlight key items:**
   Mark or write down the items you're working with to keep track of possibilities and connections.

9. **Make notes:**
   Write down possibilities or non-possibilities in the graph.

10. **Stay systematic:**
Identify the category with the fewest blanks or unknowns and focus on solving it first—it often unlocks the rest of the puzzle.

11. **Pay attention to names:**
Be careful not to mix up similar names.

12. **Place information carefully:**
Make sure the correct details go in the correct box or category.

13. **Double-check:**
Confirm your solution matches *all* the clues.

Train Your Brain - Level 3 - Book 1 - Logic Puzzle # 1 Clues

1. Pam's favorite Broadway show is *Shadows on Fifth.*
2. Chris' favorite Broadway song is not "Just Say Curtain."
3. Naomi's favorite Broadway song is "Stuck Between the Stars."
4. The woman whose favorite Broadway show is *Bright Lights* wears a Broadway T-shirt when she goes to the show.
5. Eliza's favorite Broadway song is "This Street Remembers," but she does not wear a Broadway T-shirt when she goes to her favorite show.
6. The woman whose favorite Broadway song is "Do You Hear the Marigolds" wears a red sash to her favorite show.
7. Linda's favorite Broadway show is *The Waltz*.
8. Pam wears a sequined dress when she goes to her favorite show.
9. Linda's favorite Broadway song is "Do You Hear the Marigolds."
10. The woman whose favorite Broadway song is "Laugh" also loves the Broadway show *Twelve Ghosts*.
11. Angie's favorite Broadway show is *Velvet and Ashes*.
12. Chris always wears green glitter to her favorite show.
13. The woman whose favorite Broadway song is "Half Past Always" wears a black silk dress to her favorite show.
14. The woman whose favorite Broadway show is *The Clockmaker* wears a velvet cloak to the show.

Train Your Brain - Level 3 - Book 1 - Logic Puzzle # 1

	Angie	Eliza	Pam	Naomi	Linda	Chris
Favorite Broadway Show						
Favorite Thing to Wear to the Show						
Favorite Broadway Song						

Train Your Brain - Level 3 - Book 1 - Logic Puzzle # 2 Clues

1. Someone likes glazed donuts.
2. Kelly and Nicole each have two cats.
3. The woman who wants to go on a ski vacation has no chickens.
4. Ingrid wants to go on a cruise for her vacation.
5. Leslie and Rachel have no cats.
6. The woman who likes donuts with sprinkles has two cats.
7. Ingrid does not like chocolate or maple donuts.
8. The woman who wants to go on a Mediterranean vacation eats chocolate donuts.
9. The woman who has one chicken wants to go on a safari vacation.
10. Kelly wants to go on a beach vacation.
11. Someone has two chickens and no cats.
12. Leslie does not eat chocolate donuts.
13. Rachel and Nicole have no chickens.
14. The woman who eats raspberry-filled donuts wants to go on a beach vacation.
15. Leslie has one chicken, and Kelly has three chickens.

Train Your Brain - Level 3 - Book 1 - Logic Puzzle # 2

	Leslie	Kelly	Nicole	Ingrid	Rachel
Donut					
Animals					
Type of Vacation					

Train Your Brain - Level 3 - Book 1 - Logic Puzzle # 3 Clues

1. Ethan has to stop at the bank before driving his RV on his road trip.

2. The man who likes to chew gum while driving needs to pack sunglasses.

3. David likes to snack on chips while driving.

4. The man who drives a truck does not need to pack sunscreen.

5. Mark needs to stop at the grocery store to pick up pistachios.

6. The man who needs to pack fishing gear does not eat pretzels while traveling.

7. Jeremy drives an SUV and needs to pack sandals.

8. The man who snacks on licorice while driving needs to stop at the pharmacy.

9. The man who drives a van needs to pack his fishing gear but doesn't need to get gas.

10. Ryan needs to wash his car and pack his hat.

11. The man who drives a motorcycle needs to pack sunscreen.

Train Your Brain - Level 3 - Book 1 - Logic Puzzle # 3

	Ethan	David	Mark	Jeremy	Ryan
Item to Pack for Road Trip					
Errand					
Snack for Road Trip					
Vehicle					

Train Your Brain - Level 3 - Book 1 - Logic Puzzle # 4 Clues

1. Eden photographs wildlife.
2. The woman who uses a FocusPro camera photographs historical buildings.
3. One woman uses slide film and backlighting.
4. Alexa uses a Lumenix camera and soft light.
5. The woman who uses stage lighting does not use a BrightCam camera.
6. Gabrielle uses black-and-white film and photographs products for advertisements.
7. The woman who uses a Summit camera does not photograph concerts.
8. The woman who uses color film photographs weddings.
9. One woman uses studio lighting with her Summit camera.
10. Julie uses negative film and natural light.
11. Liz uses instant film with her Clearpoint camera.

Train Your Brain - Level 3 - Book 1 - Logic Puzzle # 4

	Eden	Julie	Liz	Gabrielle	Alexa
Type of Camera					
Type of Film					
What They Photograph					
Type of Lighting					

Train Your Brain - Level 3 - Book 1 - Logic Puzzle # 5 Clues

1. The person who eats almonds as their movie treat doesn't watch movies at Big Screen Theaters or Star Cinema.

2. Louis watches movies at Film Spot and eats caramels.

3. Ava watches thriller movies and eats licorice, not popcorn.

4. The person who enjoys romance movies eats caramels.

5. Charlie watches western movies at Movie Town.

6. The person who eats chocolate bars enjoys science fiction movies at Main Street Movies.

7. Sam watches comedies at Big Screen Theaters but does not like chocolate bars.

8. The person who watches movies at Trolley North Theaters enjoys action movies and eats nachos.

9. Chuck does not watch movies at Main Street Movies.

Train Your Brain - Level 3 - Book 1 - Logic Puzzle # 5

	Evan	Sam	Louis	Charlie	Ava	Chuck
Preferred Movie Genre						
Movie Treat						
Movie Theater						

Train Your Brain - Level 3 - Book 1 - Logic Puzzle # 6 Clues

1. The hamster does not play with glitter balls.
2. Andy and his rabbit play at Lake Park.
3. Cocoa plays in cardboard tunnels.
4. The hamster and its owner play at Skyline Park.
5. Bubbles is Maya's pet fish.
6. Ben and his pet Sushi play at Maplewood Park.
7. The person who plays at North Park has a pet named Dori.
8. Someone's cat loves to play with stuffed mice.
9. Eric's pet plays with a tug rope.
10. The person who plays at Riverside Park does not have a dog.
11. Ellie's pet, Magnolia, loves to play with squeaky toys.

Train Your Brain - Level 3 - Book 1 - Logic Puzzle # 6

	Eric	Maya	Ben	Ellie	Andy
Type of Pet					
Pet's Name					
Pet's Favorite Toy					
Favorite Park					

Train Your Brain - Level 3 - Book 1 - Logic Puzzle # 7 Clues

1. Athena is not the goddess of the Hunt and Nature or of the Harvest.
2. The goddess whose sacred animal is the owl is the goddess of Wisdom.
3. Athena's symbol is not the dove.
4. One goddess has the same object as both her symbol and sacred animal.
5. Demeter's offering is not pomegranate.
6. Aphrodite is the goddess of Love and Beauty, but her sacred animal is not the deer.
7. Artemis is not the goddess of Wisdom or the Harvest.
8. Artemis' offering is honey cakes.
9. Aphrodite gives flowers as an offering, not bread.
10. The goddess of the Harvest has the wheat sheaf as her symbol, not the dove.
11. Demeter's sacred animal is the snake, not the deer or dove.
12. The goddess of the Hunt and Nature has the bow and arrow as her symbol, not the olive branch.

Train Your Brain - Level 3 - Book 1 - Logic Puzzle # 7

	Athena	Artemis	Demeter	Aphrodite
Symbol				
Offering				
Sacred Animal				
What They are the God Of				

Train Your Brain - Level 3 - Book 1 - Logic Puzzle # 8 Clues

1. Tate owns a Ridgeway bike, but he's never ridden the Cascade Classic bike trail.
2. Mae does not ride in North Carolina.
3. Ruby rides the Summit Stride bike trail.
4. The TrailBlazer bike trail is not located in Belgium.
5. Someone rides their True Gear bike on the Red Ridge bike trail.
6. Mae owns an Iron Trail bike.
7. The person who owns a Summit bike rides in New Zealand.
8. Mae rides the Sprint Series bike trail.
9. The person who owns a Velton bike rides in Canada.
10. Jane rides the Iron Peak bike trail.
11. Fred owns a Summit bike, not a Cascade bike.
12. San Diego is where the Iron Peak bike trail is located.
13. The Red Ridge bike trail is in Moab.

Train Your Brain - Level 3 - Book 1 - Logic Puzzle # 8

	Jane	Fred	Mae	Ruby	Tate	Myrna
Type of Bike They Own						
Bike Trail Where They Ride						
Location of Bike Trail						

Train Your Brain - Level 3 - Book 1 - Logic Puzzle # 9 Clues

1. Cactus Radio was popular during the late-60s to 70s, but they do not play grunge-style music.
2. The hair-metal band was inspired by Arena Rock.
3. Blue Hour was not inspired by the Delta Blues.
4. False North was famous for their pop-rock music style.
5. The hard-rock band was not inspired by British Blues.
6. One band, popular in the late-70s to 80s, was inspired by Arena Rock.
7. Blue Hour was popular from the mid-70s to 80s.
8. The band that was popular in the early 90s was inspired by Garage Bands.
9. Blue Hour was known for their soft-rock music style.
10. The band that was popular in the 60s was inspired by Rhythm and Blues.
11. Tin Can was inspired by Opera music.
12. Bloom was popular in the early 90s, not 70s to 80s.
13. The Opera-inspired band is known for glam rock.

Train Your Brain - Level 3 - Book 1 - Logic Puzzle # 9

	Tin Can	Bloom	Blue Hour	False North	Cactus Radio	Moon Seed
When They were Popular						
Style of Music						
One of Their Musical Inspirations						

Train Your Brain - Level 3 - Book 1 - Logic Puzzle # 10 Clues

1. The person who likes folk music also enjoys building blocks.
2. Gracie likes pop music.
3. Miriam does not enjoy baking.
4. The person who likes disco music also enjoys making soap.
5. Maggie and Susan both wear anklets.
6. Amy wears rings and likes to do card tricks.
7. Susan does not like indie rock.
8. The person who wears rings does not like Fudge Fusion chocolate bars.
9. The person who likes Toffee Tango chocolate bars wears necklaces, not earrings.
10. Maggie does not like Berry Bliss or Velvet Truffle chocolate bars.
11. The person who likes punk rock also enjoys Berry Bliss chocolate bars.
12. Maggie enjoys soap making, and Gracie enjoys sewing.
13. Susan does not enjoy building blocks.
14. The person who likes pop music also enjoys Hazelnut Whirl chocolate bars.

Train Your Brain - Level 3 - Book 1 - Logic Puzzle # 10

	Gracie	Miriam	Maggie	Susan	Amy
Chocolate Bar					
Jewelry					
Hobby					
Music Genre					

Train Your Brain - Level 3 - Book 1 - Logic Puzzle # 11 Clues

1. The fawn-colored dog won Reserve Best in Show.
2. Virginia's dog is a Great Dane.
3. The blue-colored dog is not a Beagle and did not win Best of Breed.
4. The tri-colored dog attended the Regal Dog Show.
5. Susannah's dog won Best of Breed.
6. The Doberman attended the Paws and Tails Dog Show.
7. Dee's Beagle won Group Winner, not Best in Show.
8. Bessie's sable-colored poodle often gets confused with Florence's fawn-colored dog.
9. Dee's dog did not attend the Noble Hound Dog Show.
10. Bessie's dog did not win Best Puppy.
11. Susannah's dog did not attend the Distinguished Pup Dog Show.
12. The Poodle attended the Grand Paws Dog Show.
13. The Afghan Hound is brindle, not fawn, in color.

Train Your Brain - Level 3 - Book 1 - Logic Puzzle # 11

	Dog Breed	Dog Color	Award Earned	Dog Show Name
Bessie				
Dee				
Florence				
Susannah				
Virginia				

Train Your Brain - Level 3 - Book 1 - Logic Puzzle # 12 Clues

1. The Greek God who wears a helmet also wears red robes.
2. Apollo eats olives and feta cheese.
3. The Greek God who plays the lyre does not eat grilled fish or wear green robes.
4. Poseidon is not the God of Travel.
5. The Greek God who holds a trident is the God of the Sea.
6. Hermes wears green robes.
7. Zeus does not wear white robes.
8. The Greek God who eats roast boar is the God of War.
9. Poseidon eats grilled fish and wears blue robes, not gold robes like another Greek God.
10. The Greek God who eats ambrosia wears gold robes and holds a thunderbolt, but they do not wear a helmet like Ares.
11. Hermes is not the God of Music.
12. The Greek God who eats ambrosia is the God of the Sky.
13. The Greek God who eats honey cakes wears winged sandals, but does not hold a trident.

Train Your Brain - Level 3 - Book 1 - Logic Puzzle # 12

	Favorite Food	Item the Greek God Holds, Wears, or Plays	Robe Color	What They are the God Of
Zeus				
Poseidon				
Ares				
Hermes				
Apollo				

Train Your Brain - Level 3 - Book 1 - Logic Puzzle # 13 Clues

1. The man who prefers to wear flip-flops has 2 siblings.
2. Nolan, who wished to be a zookeeper when he was a child, is not considered to be the most “intelligent” person.
3. The “compassionate” person prefers to wear slides.
4. Bradford does not have 1 or 3 siblings, but there is one man who has 1 sibling and another who has 3 siblings.
5. Hudson, who is “adventurous”, prefers to wear sandals.
6. The “helpful” man wished to get a kitten as a child.
7. Hudson and Bradford had the same childhood wish.
8. Lex has 4 siblings.
9. The man with no siblings wished to swim with dolphins as a child.
10. One of the men who wished to be taller as a child has only 1 sibling.
11. Bradford, who wished to be taller when he was a child, is considered to be “compassionate”.
12. Walter, a “creative” man, does not have 5 siblings.
13. Nate, who is considered to be “helpful” prefers to wear boots.
14. The man who wished to be an astronaut as a child has a personality trait other than “gentle” and does not prefer wearing dress shoes.
15. Lex prefers to wear slippers.

Train Your Brain - Level 3 - Book 1 - Logic Puzzle # 13

	Hudson	Nolan	Nate	Lex	Bradford	Walter
Personality Trait						
Favorite Shoe						
Childhood Wish						
Number of Siblings						

Train Your Brain - Level 3 - Book 1 - Logic Puzzle # 14 Clues

1. Willa's last name is Cather and she has 1 brother and 2 sisters.
2. The woman whose last name is Bronte lives in West Yorkshire.
3. Louisa's favorite book is *Little Women* and her last name is not Woolf.
4. The woman who lives in Sussex has 2 brothers and 1 sister and loves *A Room With a View.*
5. The woman who loves *Pride and Prejudice* has 6 brothers and 1 sister.
6. Charlotte's last name is Bronte.
7. Jane does not live in Scotland.
8. The woman who loves *A Lost Lady* lives in Alabama.
9. The woman who has 1 brother and 4 sisters loves reading *Jane Eyre.*
10. Mary loves *Frankenstein* and has no siblings.
11. The woman who has 7 siblings has the last name Austen and reads *Pride and Prejudice*.
12. Louisa Alcott lives in Wallingford, England and has 1 brother and 1 sister.
13. The woman whose last name is Shelley lives in Scotland.
14. Virginia lives in Sussex, unlike another woman who lives in Hampshire, England.

Train your Brain - Level 3 - Book 1 - Logic Puzzle # 14

	Jane	Mary	Virginia	Louisa	Charlotte	Willa
Siblings						
Last Name						
Favorite Book						
Where They Live						

Train your Brain - Level 3 - Book 1 - Logic Puzzle # 15 Clues

1. The person who drove 9 hours listened to “Beyond” as they traveled.
2. Gloria drove 19 hours to her destination.
3. The person who drove to Asheville drove one hour less than the longest drive.
4. One person snacked on beef jerky and listened to “Passport” while they drove.
5. Sasha’s road-trip song was “The Road I Do Not Know”.
6. One person drove to Austin, snacked on string cheese and listened to “City Lights”.
7. Issa did not listen to “Lost in a Dream” on her trip.
8. Margot drove 3.5 hours to Moab.
9. Kate drove to Asheville and snacked on granola bars.
10. One person drove 25 hours to their destination.
11. The person who traveled to Santa Fe did not listen to “The Road I Do Not Know”.
12. Issa drove to Savannah while snacking on crackers and listening to “Open Skies”.
13. Ken did not drive to Nashville but he did snack on trail mix.
14. The person who drove to Nashville and snacked on apples did not drive 31 hours.

Train Your Brain - Level 3 - Book 1 - Logic Puzzle # 15

	Ken	Margot	Sasha	Gloria	Issa	Kate
Road Trip Destination						
Snacks They Ate						
Hours They Drove						
Travel Song						

Train Your Brain - Level 3 - Book 1 - Logic Puzzle # 16 Clues

1. The monarch who ate peacock pie lived in Windsor Castle.
2. Emperor Akbar ate saffron rice with lamb.
3. Marie Antoinette was known for bathing in donkey milk to maintain youthful skin.
4. One monarch reigned in England.
5. The monarch known for wearing high heels with red soles lived in the Palace of Versailles.
6. Catherine the Great lived in Neuschwanstein Castle.
7. The Scottish monarch, known for having 1,000 chefs, lived in Edinburgh Castle.
8. Queen Elizabeth did not live in Chateau de Chambord
9. King Louis XIV, who reigned in France like another monarch, ate roasted boar with honey.
10. One of the monarchs ate marzipan sculptures.
11. Emperor Nero, who reigned in Turkey, lived in Topkapi Palace and was known for traveling with a personal chocolate maker.
12. Queen Elizabeth did not reign in Germany but was known for always wearing pale makeup.
13. The French monarch ate rosewater custard with candied violets.
14. The German monarch known for keeping a pet bear at court did not eat dormice stuffed with nuts and herbs.

Train Your Brain - Level 3 - Book 1 - Logic Puzzle # 16

	Queen Elizabeth	Louis XIV	Catherine the Great	Emperor Akbar	Emperor Nero	Marie Antoinette
Where They Reigned						
Something They are Known For						
Food They Ate						
Castle They Lived In						

Train Your Brain - Level 3 - Book 1 - Logic Puzzle # 17 Clues

1. The woman whose last name is McNeil loves huckleberry-flavored ice cream topped with strawberries from her garden.

2. The man who likes to make lasagna has the last name Hall.

3. Jeffrey does not have the last name Johnson.

4. Lisa grows red peppers and loves to make chicken pot pie.

5. Kent Casper grows zucchini and likes to make curry.

6. Daxton and Kent both love chocolate ice cream.

7. Brooke's last name is Lee.

8. The person with the last name Johnson loves pistachio-flavored ice cream.

9. Jeffrey plants carrots in his garden and loves to smoke ribs.

10. Daxton does not grow lettuce in his garden.

11. The woman who loves vanilla ice cream does not plant tomatoes in her garden and does not like to cook stir fry.

12. Brooke likes to make enchiladas.

13. Alicia does not have the last name Casper or Esperson and does not like caramel-flavored ice cream.

Train Your Brain - Level 3 - Book 1 - Logic Puzzle # 17

	Kent	Brooke	Alicia	Daxton	Lisa	Jeffrey
What They Plant in Their Garden						
Favorite Meal to Prepare						
Favorite Ice Cream Flavor						
Last Name						

Train Your Brain - Level 3 - Book 1 - Logic Puzzle # 18 Clues

1. Books for Everyone and Minimal Life both have a manager named Mary.

2. Fox's Flowers is open between 9 am and 6 pm and sells flowers.

3. Czechia's Treats, managed by Riana, offers a sale on baker's dozen Kolaches and is open between 6:30 am and 1:00 pm

4. The book shop has a special sale on stationery.

5. Collect Me sells thrifted clothes.

6. Minimal Life does not have a dozen-roses sale, but another store does.

7. Skateboard Shop is open between 10 am and 8 pm and sells skateboards.

8. The store that is open between 9 am and 6 pm is managed by Dirk.

9. Collect Me has a buy 1 get 1 free (B1G1) sale on shirts.

10. The store with skater shoes 20 % off is managed by Stephanie.

11. Books For Everyone is not open between 1 pm and 9 pm.

12. One of the stores sells plants.

13. The store managed by Darin is not open between 12 pm and 8 pm.

14. Minimal Life, open between 11 am and 5 pm, has a buy 2 get 1 free (B2G1) sale on ceramics.

Train Your Brain - Level 3 - Book 1 - Logic Puzzle # 18

	Skateboard Shop	Books for Everyone	Czechia's Treats	Collect Me	Minimal Life	Fox's Flowers
Hours						
Manager Name						
Popular Item Sold						
Special Sale						

Train Your Brain - Level 3 - Book 1 - Logic Puzzle # 19 Clues

1. The person who went to London for a senior trip attended Brighton High School and is planning to attend the University of Utah (U of U).
2. The man working as a lifeguard for the summer went to Florida for his senior trip.
3. Deborah is interning at a hospital for the summer.
4. Michael didn't go to the beach or Las Vegas for his senior trip, but others did.
5. Kimball attended Orem High School and is installing pools for a summer job.
6. The person who attended Timpview High School is going to Brigham Young University (BYU).
7. Kimball and Michael are both going to Harvard.
8. Deborah went to the beach for her senior trip.
9. The person who went to Paris for their senior trip is going to Harvard.
10. Jackson, who will attend University of California, Los Angeles (UCLA), did not attend Mountain View High School.
11. The Provo High School graduate is mowing lawns for the summer.
12. The woman who is attending Utah Valley University (UVU) did not attend Timpanogos High School and is not working as a guitar teacher for the summer.
13. Michael graduated from Provo High School and went to Italy for his senior trip.
14. Karla, who graduated from Timpview High school, is working as a nanny for the summer.

Train Your Brain - Level 3 - Book 1 - Logic Puzzle # 19

	Jackson	Cynthia	Deborah	Kimball	Karla	Michael
Senior Trip						
High School						
Summer Plans						
College						

1. Jared runs the 100-meter dash.
2. Tiffany never drinks chocolate milk after a race, but someone does.
3. Ashley eats spaghetti the day before running the 800-meter race.
4. One woman wears a blue and yellow uniform, eats oatmeal with fruit before racing and then eats fruit and nuts after racing.
5. Ashley and Tiffany both wear red uniforms.
6. Jared eats a bagel with peanut butter after racing.
7. The person who runs the 400-meter hurdles likes cheese and raisins after racing, eats pesto pasta before racing, and wears a blue uniform.
8. The woman who races in the 200-meter race eats veggies and hummus after racing.
9. Someone eats yogurt after racing.
10. Amy wears a green uniform.
11. One of the women who wears a red uniform eats chicken alfredo before racing in the 4x400-meter relay.
12. The man who wears an orange uniform eats lasagna before his race.
13. Landon does not eat a turkey sandwich before racing.
14. Lydia eats oatmeal with fruit before racing in the 1500-meter race.

	Ashley	Amy	Lydia	Jared	Tiffany	Landon
Food Before Race						
Track Event						
Uniform Color						
Snack After Race						

Train Your Brain - Level 3 - Book 1 - Logic Puzzle # 21 Clues

1. Joey's best school subject is math, and he enjoys doing math homework every day.
2. Ellie doesn't play the tuba and never wanted to be a rock star.
3. Jace cleans the bathroom before doing his history homework.
4. The person who cleans the kitchen counters enjoys writing papers for English, is a good writer, and dreamed of becoming an author as a child.
5. Ellie and Jace both wanted to be doctors as children.
6. Joey has a black belt in karate.
7. The person who plays the drums vacuums and then finishes his biology homework.
8. The person who does chemistry homework is really good with numbers.
9. The girl who wanted to be a doctor is good at art.
10. Jacob, who wanted to be a firefighter as a child, does not take out the garbage.
11. The person who sweeps the kitchen floor does physics homework.
12. The person who wanted to be a lawyer as a child takes out the garbage.
13. One of the people who wanted to be a doctor sweeps the kitchen floor.
14. Max isn't good with numbers and does not mow the lawn.
15. Kate cleans the kitchen counters before writing her English paper.

Train Your Brain - Level 3 - Book 1 - Logic Puzzle # 21

	Joey	Ellie	Jacob	Jace	Kate	Max
Talent						
Chore						
Homework						
Dream Job as a Child						

Train Your Brain - Level 3 - Book 1 - Logic Puzzle # 22 Clues

1. Frederik owns Hearst Castle, the newest historic home, built in 1947.
2. Two homes were built in 1895.
3. The Breakers historic home is not a $7 million, 21,000-square-foot home, but one of the homes is.
4. Charles owns Mount Vernon, a Colonial-style home.
5. Harold does not own a Victorian-style home.
6. Alexander's historic home is 178,926 square feet.
7. The Neoclassical-style home was built in 1772, not 1758.
8. The Biltmore Estate cost $150 million.
9. Charles' home was not built in 1895.
10. Harold's home is the least expensive and smallest.
11. Willem owns a Renaissance-style home that cost $35 million.
12. The $5 million home is 11,000 square feet.
13. Someone owns a Mediterranean-style home that cost $191 million, and is 68,500 square feet.
14. The Monticello historic home is not a 62,482-square-foot home.

Train Your Brain - Level 3 - Book 1 - Logic Puzzle # 22

	Historic Home Name	Style of Home	Year Built	Estimated Cost	Square Footage
Harold					
Charles					
Alexander					
Willem					
Frederik					

Train Your Brain - Level 3 - Book 1 - Logic Puzzle # 23 Clues

1. Rachel's cat is named after her favorite yellow fruit.
2. Carl's cat and her only two kittens do not live in a barn or in a townhouse.
3. Molly has two black kittens and one tortoiseshell kitten.
4. Nox enjoys watching birds from her apartment window.
5. The cat who lives in a barn has three kittens, and they all love playing with mice.
6. At the park where they live, a mother cat plays with her two tuxedo kittens.
7. Lemon has two white kittens and two black kittens who love playing fetch.
8. Scout lives at a park and plays with string.
9. Marie's cat has the shortest name.
10. The two calico kittens and one Siamese kitten do not live at the park or in a barn.

Train Your Brain - Level 3 - Book 1 - Logic Puzzle # 23

	Brian	Carl	Marie	Rachel
Mother Cat's Name				
Number and Coloring of Kittens				
Where the Cat and Her Kittens Live				
Cats' Favorite Activity				

Train Your Brain - Level 3 - Book 1 - Logic Puzzle # 24 Clues

1. Finley owns a fish.
2. Someone owns a cat and grows tulips.
3. Rowan owns a dog.
4. Mable and her partner, Alan, grow marigolds.
5. Judy owns a guinea pig.
6. Charlie grows edelweiss.
7. Judy and Steve grow ferns.
8. Mark's partner is Karen.
9. Mable owns a horse.
10. Alan does not own a cat.
11. Blake plays with her dog.
12. Someone owns a dog and grows hostas.
13. Taylor grows cornflowers.
14. Jordan takes their pet monkey to the vet.

Train Your Brain - Level 3 - Book 1 - Logic Puzzle # 24

	Judy	Finley	Mable	Rowan	Taylor	Mark
Plant/ Flower They Grow						
Partner's Name						
Pet						

Train Your Brain - Level 3 - Book 1 - Logic Puzzle # 25 Clues

1. The person who drinks cola likes oatmeal raisin cookies.
2. Kate does not like turkey and cheese sandwiches.
3. The person who eats ham sandwiches drinks root beer.
4. The person who likes roast beef sandwiches likes veggie chips.
5. Kate likes lemon bars, and Marianne likes chocolate chip cookies.
6. Penny drinks lemonade.
7. Georgia does not like corn chips or peanut butter cookies.
8. Marianne likes root beer.
9. The person who drinks orange soda likes lemon bars.
10. The person who likes turkey and cheese sandwiches drinks grape soda.
11. Kate and Harriet like potato chips.
12. Penny likes tortilla chips and sugar cookies.
13. Georgia does not like meatball subs.
14. The person who likes tortilla chips likes veggie sandwiches.

Train Your Brain - Level 3 - Book 1 - Logic Puzzle # 25

	Marianne	Georgia	Kate	Harriet	Penny
Sandwich					
Chips					
Cookie					
Drink					

Train Your Brain - Level 3 - Book 1 - Logic Puzzle # 26 Clues

1. Hugh's horse is named after something that grows in a flower garden.
2. Kate's horse is black.
3. Chad's horse is a Quarter Pony, and is second to smallest in height.
4. Ava's horse's breed has a state name in it.
5. Ann has always wanted an Arabian or Fjord horse, but she doesn't have either yet.
6. The Quarter Horse, not the Quarter Pony, is 15.5 hands tall.
7. The horse named Rose is dun in color, but not silver dun.
8. The sorrel-colored horse is 2.5 hands taller than the horse named Mesquite.
9. Hugh has the smallest horse at 13 hands tall.
10. The Arabian horse is 15.2 hands.
11. Kate's horse is not 14.5 hands, but one of the horses is.
12. Aspen, a Tennessee Walker, is 4 hands taller than Hugh's horse.
13. The black horse is named Tom, not Finale.
14. Finale is a bay-colored Quarter Horse.

Train Your Brain - Level 3 - Book 1 - Logic Puzzle # 26

	Horse Breed	Horse Name	Horse Color	Horse Height in "Hands"
Ava				
Chad				
Ann				
Kate				
Hugh				

Train Your Brain - Level 3 - Book 1 - Logic Puzzle # 27 Clues

1. Garrett's middle name is Peter and he has 2 brothers.
2. James' favorite book is *The Count of Monte Cristo* and his middle name is not Matthew.
3. The boy who lives in Pleasant Grove has 1 brother and 1 sister and loves *Adventures of Huckleberry Finn.*
4. The boy whose middle name is Andrew lives in the Ivory Coast.
5. The boy who never reads has 3 brothers and 1 sister.
6. Zach's middle name is Tyler.
7. Aaron doesn't live in the Ivory Coast or Spanish Fork.
8. The boy who loves *A Tale of Two Cities* lives in Orem.
9. The boy who has 1 brother and 2 sisters loves reading *Three Musketeers.*
10. Max loves *Treasure Island* and is the oldest of 5 kids.
11. The boy who has 4 siblings has the middle name Richard and he does not have a favorite book because he never reads.
12. James David lives in Provo and has the same number of siblings as Garrett.
13. The boy named after his dad, Tyler, lives in Spanish Fork.
14. Clark lives in Pleasant Grove, unlike someone else who lives in Tampa.

Train Your Brain - Level 3 - Book 1 - Logic Puzzle # 27

	Aaron	Max	Clark	James	Zach	Garrett
Siblings						
Middle Name						
Favorite Book						
Where They Live						

Train Your Brain - Level 3 - Book 1 - Logic Puzzle # 28 Clues

1. Bill won the Solaris Cup in his yellow car.
2. The woman who drives a white Glacia did not win the Aurora Grand Prix, but she did win a different race.
3. Pam's team manager, Sam, teases her about driving the same type of car for races and everyday driving.
4. George won the Titan 24 and then had his manager, Ty, drive him home in his non-racing car, a Daton.
5. Matt won the Crimson Circuit in his orange Stratos.
6. The woman who drives a red Luminex won the Phoenix Classic.
7. Steve enjoys driving around town in his Magnus with his manager, Jeff.
8. Matt dreams of racing in Azure Rally, but his manager, Parker, hasn't been able to help make it happen.
9. The person who races in a Blaze GT doesn't get along with the team manager, Jake.
10. The person who drives a Tigra every day does not have a green race car.
11. One man drives a blue Azurebolt.
12. The Phantom's owner's name and car color start with the same letter.
13. After winning Azure Rally, the driver left the race with Dave in their everyday car, a Stellar.
14. The person who drives a black Madra on a regular basis races in an orange car.

Train Your Brain - Level 3 - Book 1 - Logic Puzzle # 28

	Pam	George	Bill	Matt	Kendra	Steve
Race car						
Color of Race Car						
Race						
Team Manager						
Everyday Car						

Train Your Brain - Level 3 - Book 1 - Logic Puzzle # 29 Clues

1. The person who bought a new fridge after going to the zoo is Christian.
2. The Native Hawaiian man likes to visit the Pokemon store.
3. Abby is Caucasian.
4. Nathan does not like to watch sports on TV or attend sporting events.
5. Cameron is Buddhist and Korean.
6. The practicing Jewish person is shopping for a new washing machine.
7. Noah and Nathan bought the same new appliance.
8. Abby finished making a quilt.
9. The person who watches soccer on TV had to buy a new oven instead of a bigger TV.
10. Noah is not Catholic.
11. The Muslim is African American.
12. The woman who bought a new microwave does not practice Confucianism and is not Samoan.
13. Nathan is Muslim and spends more time reading books than watching his new TV.
14. Bridgette does not like to read or go to basketball games.
15. Emily is Jewish and Ethiopian.

Train Your Brain - Level 3 - Book 1 - Logic Puzzle # 29

	Cameron	Noah	Emily	Abby	Nathan	Bridgette
Religion						
Ethnicity						
New Appliance						
Activity						

Train Your Brain - Level 3 - Book 1 - Logic Puzzle # 30 Clues

1. The person whose favorite part of therapy is getting a massage has the last name Benson and 3 children.
2. The Dutch man likes cognitive therapy.
3. Kayla is Italian.
4. Matthew does not like vision therapy or sound mapping therapy.
5. Brandon Nelson is Swedish.
6. The person with the last name Jones has 2 kids.
7. Brandon and Matthew both have 4 children.
8. Kayla's favorite part of therapy is brainwaves.
9. The person who loves vision therapy has 4 children.
10. Jim has 1 child and does not have the last name Davis.
11. Mr. Clayton is Canadian.
12. The woman who has no children does not have the last name Hansen and is not French.
13. Matthew Clayton has 4 children and enjoys doing cardio therapy.
14. Mary Jones is American.

Train Your Brain - Level 3 - Book 1 - Logic Puzzle # 30

	Brandon	Jim	Mary	Kayla	Matthew	Rachelle
Last Name						
Number of Children						
Nationality						
Favorite Part of Therapy						

Train Your Brain - Level 3 - Book 1 - Logic Puzzle # 31 Clues

1. The slowest car has a top speed of 124 mph (199 kph).
2. The Kanzai and Veltrix both have the same engine volume, which is less than the 2.5 liters of another car.
3. Wyatt's car does not have a 5.7 liter engine or a 1.6 liter engine.
4. Zachary's car is the second most expensive car.
5. Wyatt loves pushing his car to its top speed of 162 mph (261 kph).
6. Zachary drives the newest car.
7. The least expensive and oldest car has the highest volume engine.
8. William's car is the most expensive car, costing $2,720,000.
9. Someone owns a Rheinberg sports car.
10. Garrett drives the slowest of the cars.
11. The most expensive car is also the fastest car, with a top speed of 219 mph (352 kph).
12. Caden's car doesn't cost $128,600 or $11,194.
13. Wyatt and Garrett's cars were built in the 1980s, with Garrett's car being four years older than Wyatt's.
14. The 1969 Stallion doesn't drive 190 mph (305 kph).
15. The least expensive car cost $4,781, much less than another car that cost $43,350.
16. Two cars have 1.6 liter engines.
17. The 2025 Vortex has a 4 liter engine.
18. The 1988 car doesn't drive 190 mph (305 kph) or 170 mph (273 kph).
19. Caden drives the oldest and least expensive car.
20. William's Veltrix is three years older than Zachary's 2025 car.
21. Wyatt's car is just over four times more expensive than Garrett's car.
22. Caden's car was not built in 1988 or 1984.

Train Your Brain - Level 3 - Book 1 - Logic Puzzle # 31

	Car	Year	Cost of Car	Top Speed	Engine Volume (Liters)
Zachary					
Wyatt					
Caden					
Garrett					
William					

TRAIN YOUR BRAIN LOGIC PUZZLES
ANSWER KEY

Train Your Brain - Level 3 - Book 1 - Logic Puzzle # 1

	Angie	Eliza	Pam	Naomi	Linda	Chris
Favorite Broadway Show	Velvet And Ashes	The Clockmaker	Shadows On Fifth	Bright Lights	The Waltz	Twelve Ghosts
Favorite Thing To Wear To The Show	Black Silk Dress	Velvet Cloak	Sequined Dress	Broadway T-Shirt	Red Sash	Green Glitter
Favorite Broadway Song	Half Past Always	This Street Remembers	Just Say Curtain	Stuck Between The Stars	Do You Hear The Marigolds	Laugh

Train Your Brain - Level 3 - Book 1 - Logic Puzzle # 2

	Leslie	Kelly	Nicole	Ingrid	Rachel
Donut	Maple	Raspberry-Filled Donuts	Sprinkles	Glazed	Chocolate
Animals	0 Cats 1 Chicken	2 Cats 3 Chickens	2 Cats 0 Chickens	0 Cats 2 Chicken	0 Cats 0 Chickens
Type Of Vacation	Safari	Beach	Ski	Cruise	Mediterranean

Train Your Brain - Level 3 - Book 1 - Logic Puzzle # 3

	Ethan	David	Mark	Jeremy	Ryan
Item To Pack	Sunglasses	Sunscreen	Fishing Gear	Sandals	Hat
Errand	Bank	Get Gas	Grocery Store	Pharmacy	Wash Car
Snack For Road Trip	Gum	Chips	Pistachios	Licorice	Pretzels
Vehicle	Rv	Motorcycle	Van	SUV	Truck

Train Your Brain - Level 3 - Book 1 - Logic Puzzle # 4

	Eden	Julie	Liz	Gabrielle	Alexa
Type Of Camera	Brightcam	Focuspro	Clearpoint	Summit	Lumenix
Type Of Film	Slide	Negative	Instant	Black-And-White	Color
What They Photograph	Wildlife	Historical Buildings	Concerts	Products For Advertisements	Weddings
Type Of Lighting	Backlight	Natural	Stage	Studio	Soft

Train Your Brain - Level 3 - Book 1 - Logic Puzzle # 5

	Evan	Sam	Louis	Charlie	Ava	Chuck
Preferred Movie Genre	Science Fiction	Comedy	Romance	Western	Thriller	Action
Movie Treat	Chocolate Bars	Popcorn	Caramels	Almonds	Licorice	Nachos
Movie Theater	Main Street Movies	Big Screen Theaters	Film Spot	Movie Town	Star Cinema	Trolley North Theaters

Train Your Brain - Level 3 - Book 1 - Logic Puzzle # 6

	Eric	Maya	Ben	Ellie	Andy
Type Of Pet	Dog	Fish	Cat	Hamster	Rabbit
Pet's Name	Dori	Bubbles	Sushi	Magnolia	Cocoa
Pet's Favorite Toy	Tug Rope	Glitter Balls	Stuffed Mice	Squeaky Toys	Cardboard Tunnels
Favorite Park	North Park	Riverside Park	Maplewood Park	Skyline Park	Lake Park

Train Your Brain - Level 3 - Book 1 - Logic Puzzle # 7

	Athena	Artemis	Demeter	Aphrodite
Symbol	Olive Branch	Bow And Arrow	Wheat Sheaf	Dove
Offering	Pomegranate	Honey Cakes	Bread	Flowers
Sacred Animal	Owl	Deer	Snake	Dove
What They Are The God Of	Wisdom	Hunt And Nature	Harvest	Love And Beauty

Train Your Brain - Level 3 - Book 1 - Logic Puzzle # 8

	Jane	Fred	Mae	Ruby	Tate	Myrna
Type Of Bike They Own	Cascade	Summit	Iron Trail	Velton	Ridgeway	True Gear
Favorite Bike Trail	Iron Peak	Cascade Classic	Sprint Series	Summit Stride	Trailblazer	Red Ridge
Location Of Bike Trail Where They Ride	San Diego	New Zealand	Belgium	Canada	North Carolina	Moab

Train Your Brain - Level 3 - Book 1 - Logic Puzzle # 9

	Tin Can	Bloom	Blue Hour	False North	Cactus Radio	Moonseed
When They Were Most Popular	70s - 80s	90s	Mid 70s - 80s	60s	Late 60s - 70s	Late 70s - 80s
Style Of Music	Glam Rock	Grunge	Soft Rock	Pop Rock	Hard Rock	Hair Metal
One Of Their Musical Inspirations	Opera	Garage Bands	British Blues	Rhythm And Blues	Delta Blues	Arena Rock

Train Your Brain - Level 3 - Book 1 - Logic Puzzle # 10

	Gracie	Miriam	Maggie	Susan	Amy
Chocolate Bar	Hazelnut Whirl	Toffee Tango	Fudge Fusion	Berry Bliss	Velvet Truffle

Jewelry	Earrings	Necklaces	Anklet	Anklet	Rings
Hobby	Sewing	Blocks	Soap Making	Baking	Card Tricks
Music Genre	Pop Music	Folk Music	Disco	Punk Rock	Indie Rock

Train Your Brain - Level 3 - Book 1 - Logic Puzzle # 11

	Dog Breed	Dog Color	Award Earned	Dog Show Name
Bessie	Poodle	Sable	Best In Show	Grand Paws
Dee	Beagle	Tricolor	Group Winner	Regal
Florence	Doberman	Fawn	Reserve Best In Show	Paws And Tails
Susannah	Afghan Hound	Brindle	Best Of Breed	Noble Hound
Virginia	Great Dane	Blue	Best Puppy	Distinguished Pup

Train Your Brain - Level 3 - Book 1 - Logic Puzzle # 12

	Favorite Food	Mythical Creature	Robe Color	What They Are The God Of
Zeus	Ambrosia	Thunderbot	Gold	Sky
Poseidon	Grilled Fish	Trident	Blue	Sea
Ares	Roast Boar	Helmet	Red	War
Hermes	Honey Cakes	Winged Sandals	Green	Travel
Apollo	Olives & Feta	Lyre	White	Music

Train Your Brain - Level 3 - Book 1 - Logic Puzzle # 13

	Hudson	Nolan	Nate	Lex	Bradford	Walter
Personality Trait	Adventurous	Gentle	Helpful	Intelligent	Compassionate	Creative
Shoe	Sandals	Flip Flops	Boots	Slippers	Slides	Dress Shoes
Childhood Wish	Taller	Zookeeper	Get Kitten	Astronaut	Taller	Swim With Dolphins
Siblings	1	2	3	4	5	0

Train Your Brain - Level 3 - Book 1 - Logic Puzzle # 14

	Jane	Mary	Virginia	Louisa	Charlotte	Willa
Siblings	6 Brothers 1 Sister	0	2 Brothers 1 Sister	1 Brother 1 Sister	1 Brother 4 Sisters	1 Brother 2 Sisters
Last Name	Austen	Shelley	Woolf	Alcott	Bronte	Cather
Favorite Book	*Pride And Prejudice*	*Frankenstein*	*A Room With A View*	*Little Women*	*Jane Eyre*	*A Lost Lady*
Where They Live	Hampshire England	Scotland	Sussex	Wallingford England	West Yorkshire	Alabama

Train Your Brain - Level 3 - Book 1 - Logic Puzzle # 15

	Ken	Margot	Sasha	Gloria	Issa	Kate
Road Trip Destination	Santa Fe	Moab	Nashville	Austin	Savannah	Asheville
Snacks They Ate	Trail Mix	Beef Jerky	Apples	String Cheese	Crackers	Granola Bars
Hours They Drove	9 Hours	3.5 Hours	25 Hours	19 Hours	31 Hours	30 Hours
Favorite Travel Song	Beyond	Passport	The Road I Do Not Know	City Lights	Open Skies	Lost In A Dream

Train Your Brain - Level 3 - Book 1 - Logic Puzzle # 16

	Queen Elizabeth	Louis Xiv	Catherine The Great	Emperor Akbar	Emperor Nero	Marie Antoinette
Where They Reigned	England	France	Germany	Scotland	Turkey	France
Something They Are Known For	Pale Makeup	Wore High Heels With Red Soles	Kept A Pet Bear At Court	Had 1,000 Chefs	Traveled With A Personal Chocolate Maker	Bathed In Donkey Milk For Youthful Skin
Food They Ate	Peacock Pie	Roasted Boar With Honey	Marzipan Sculptures	Saffron Rice With Lamb	Dormice Stuffed With Nuts And Herbs	Rosewater Custard With Candied Violets
Castle They Lived In	Windsor Castle	Palace Of Versailles	Neuschwanstein Castle	Edinburgh Castle	Topkapi Palace	Chateau De Chambord

Train Your Brain - Level 3 - Book 1 - Logic Puzzle # 17

	Kent	Brooke	Alicia	Daxton	Lisa	Jeffrey
Garden	Zucchini	Lettuce	Strawberries	Tomatoes	Red Peppers	Carrots
Favorite Meal	Curry	Enchiladas	Stir Fry	Lasagna	Chicken Pot Pie	Ribs
Favorite Ice Cream Flavor	Chocolate	Vanilla	Huckleberry	Chocolate	Pistachio	Caramel
Last Name	Casper	Lee	Mcneil	Hall	Johnson	Esperson

Train Your Brain - Level 3 - Book 1 - Logic Puzzle # 18

	Skateboard Shop	Books For Everyone	Czechia's Treats	Collect Me	Minimal Life	Fox's Flowers
Hours	10-8	12-8	6:30-1:00	1-9	11-5	9-6
Manager Name	Stephanie	Mary	Riana	Darin	Mary	Dirk
Most Sold Item	Skateboard	Books	Kolaches	Thrifted Clothes	Plants	Flowers
Special Sale	Vans 20% Off	Stationary 10% Off	Bakers Dozen	B1g1 On Shirts	B2g1 On Ceramics	Dozen Roses

Train Your Brain - Level 3 - Book 1 - Logic Puzzle # 19

	Jackson	Cynthia	Deborah	Kimball	Karla	Michael
Senior Trip	Florida	London	Beach	Paris	Las Vegas	Italy
High School	Timpanogos	Brighton	Mountain View	Orem	Timpview	Provo
Summer Job	Lifeguard	Teach Guitar	Hospital Intern	Install Pools	Nanny	Mow Lawns
College	UCLA	University Of Utah	Utah Valley University	Harvard	BYU	Harvard

Train Your Brain - Level 3 - Book 1 - Logic Puzzle # 20

	Ashley	Amy	Lydia	Jared	Tiffany	Landon
Meal Before Race	Spaghetti	Turkey Sandwich	Oatmeal With Fruit	Lasagna	Chicken Alfredo	Pesto Pasta
Track Event	800 M	200 M	1500 M	100 M	4 X 400 M Relay	400 M Hurdles
Uniform Color	Red	Green	Blue And Yellow	Orange	Red	Blue
Snack After Race	Chocolate Milk	Veggies & Hummus	Fruit & Nuts	Bagel With Peanut Butter	Yogurt	Cheese & Raisins

Train Your Brain - Level 3 - Book 1 - Logic Puzzle # 21

	Joey	Ellie	Jacob	Jace	Kate	Max
Talent	Karate	Good At Art	Good With Numbers	Plays Trombone	Good Writer	Plays Drums
Chore	Take Out Garbage	Sweep Kitchen Floor	Mow Lawn	Clean Bathroom	Clean Kitchen Counters	Vacuum
Homework	Math	Physics	Chemistry	History	English	Biology
Dream Job	Lawyer	Doctor	Firefighter	Doctor	Author	Rock Star

Train Your Brain - Level 3 - Book 1 - Logic Puzzle # 22

	Historic Home Name	Style Of Home	Year Built	Estimated Cost	Square Footage
Harold	Monticello	Neoclassical	1772	$5 Million	11,000
Charles	Mount Vernon	Colonial	1758	$7 Million	21,000
Alexander	Biltmore	Victorian	1895	$150 Million	178,926
Willem	The Breakers	Renaissance	1895	$35 Million	62,482
Frederik	Hearst Castle	Mediterranean	1947	$191 Million	68,500

Train Your Brain - Level 3 - Book 1 - Logic Puzzle # 23

	Brian	Carl	Marie	Rachel
Mother Cat's Name	Molly	Scout	Nox	Lemon
Number And Coloring Of Kittens	2 Black 1 Tortoise Shell	2 Tuxedo	2 Calico 1 Siamese	2 Black 2 White
Where The Cat And Her Kittens Live	Barn	Park	Apartment	Townhouse
Cats' Favorite Activity	Mice	String	Birds	Fetch

Train Your Brain - Level 3 - Book 1 Logic Puzzle # 24

	Judy	Finley	Mable	Rowan	Taylor	Mark
Plant/Flower	Ferns	Edelweiss	Marigolds	Hosta	Cornflowers	Tulips
Partner	Steve	Charlie	Alan	Blake	Jordan	Karen
Pet	Guinea Pig	Fish	Horses	Dogs	Monkey	Cats

Train Your Brain - Level 3 - Book 1 - Logic Puzzle # 25

	Marianne	Georgia	Kate	Harriet	Penny
Sandwich	Ham	Roast Beef	Meatball Sub	Turkey And Cheese	Veggie
Chips	Corn Chips	Veggie Chips	Potato Chips	Potato Chips	Tortilla Chips
Cookie	Chocolate Chip	Oatmeal Raisin	Lemon Bars	Peanut Butter Cookies	Sugar Cookies
Drink	Root Beer	Cola	Orange	Grape	Lemonade

Train Your Brain - Level 3 - Book 1 - Logic Puzzle # 26

	Horse Breed	Horse Name	Horse Color	Horse Height In Hands
Ava	Tennessee Walker	Aspen	Sorrel	17
Chad	Quarter Pony	Mesquite	Silver Dun	14.5
Ann	Quarter Horse	Finale	Bay	15.5
Kate	Arabian	Tom	Black	15.2
Hugh	Fjord	Rose	Dun	13

Train Your Brain - Level 3 - Book 1 - Logic Puzzle # 27

	Aaron	Max	Clark	James	Zach	Garrett
Siblings	4 - 3 Brothers, 1 Sister	4	2 - 1 Brother 1 Sister	2 Brothers	3 - 1 Brother 2 Sisters	2 Brothers
Middle Name	Richard	Andrew	Matthew	David	Tyler	Peter
Favorite Book	*None*	*Treasure Island*	*Adventures Of Huckleberry Finn*	*The Count Of Monte Cristo*	*Three Musketeers*	*A Tale Of Two Cities*
Where They Live	Tampa	Ivory Coast	Pleasant Grove	Provo	Spanish Fork	Orem

Train Your Brain - Level 3 - Book 1 - Logic Puzzle # 28

	Pam	George	Bill	Matt	Kendra	Steve
Race Car	Luminex	Phantom	Blaze GT	Stratos	Glacia	Azurebolt
Color Of Race Car	Red	Green	Yellow	Orange	White	Blue
Race	Phoenix Classic	Titan 24	Solaris Cup	Crimson Circuit	Azure Rally	Aurora Grand Prix
Team Manager	Sam	Ty	Jake	Parker	Dave	Jeff
Everyday Car	Luminex	Daton	Tigra	Madra	Stellar	Magnus

Train Your Brain - Level 3 - Book 1 - Logic Puzzle # 29

	Cameron	Noah	Emily	Abby	Nathan	Bridgette
Religion	Buddhist	Confucianism	Jewish	Catholic	Muslim	Christian
Ethnicity	Korean	Native Hawaiian	Ethiopian	Caucasian	African American	Samoan
New Appliance	Oven	Television	Washing Machine	Microwave	Television	Fridge
Activity	Watch Soccer Matches On Tv	Pokemon	Go To Basketball Game	Quilts	Read Books	Zoo

Train Your Brain - Level 3 - Book 1 - Logic Puzzle # 30

	Brandon	Jim	Mary	Kayla	Matthew	Rachelle
Occupation Last Name	Nelson	Hansen	Jones	Davis	Clayton	Benson
# Of Children	4	1	2	0	4	3
City/ Nationality	Swedish	Dutch	American	Italian	Canadian	French
Favorite Part Of Therapy	Vision	Cognitive Therapy	Sound Mapping	Brainwaves	Cardio	Massage

Train Your Brain - Level 3 - Book 1 - Logic Puzzle # 31

	Dream Car	Year	Cost Of Car	Top Speed	Engine Volume (Liters)
Zachary	Vortex	2025	$128,600	190 Mph 305 Kph	4 Liter
Wyatt	Rheinberg	1988	$43,350	162 Mph 261kph	2.5 Liter
Caden	Stallion	1969	$4,781	170 Mph 273 Kph	5.7 Liter
Garrett	Kanzai	1984	$11,194	124 Mph 199 Kph	1.6 Liter
William	Veltrix	2022	$2,720.00	219 Mph 352 Kph	1.6 Liter

Made in United States
North Haven, CT
06 November 2026

21861533R00041